The Craft Queen's
Guide to
Hip Knits

The Craft Queen's Guide to
Hip Knits

Catherine Tough

PHOTOGRAPHY BY CHRIS TUBBS

C&T PUBLISHING

First published in North America
by C&T Publishing Inc.,
PO Box 1456, Lafayette, CA 94549

Text and project designs copyright © Catherine Tough 2006
Photographs and illustrations copyright © Conran Octopus 2006
Book design and layout copyright © Conran Octopus 2006

British Library Cataloguing-in-Publication Data.
A catalogue record for this book is available from the British Library.

Publishing Director: Lorraine Dickey
Art Directors: Lucy Gowans and Jonathan Christie
Executive Editor: Zia Mattocks
Editor: Sybella Marlow
Designer: Nicky Barneby
Editor: Emma Clegg
Illustrator: Alice Tait
Stylist: Nicki Peters
Photographer's Assistant: Natasha Sturny
Production Manager: Angela Couchman

ISBN 978-1-57120-414-1
Printed in China

Acknowledgments

The author would like to thank everyone at Rowan for their assistance in
the preparation of this book. Also a big thank you to my family for all their
help and support.

Contents

Introduction

When asked to produce some ideas for a book entitled *The Craft Queen's Guide to Hip Knits*, I have to admit I felt a moment of alarm. For a start, until very recently knitting and 'hipness' had not been close companions since as far back as the mid-1980s. I seem to remember that then everyone seemed to be knitting batwing picture jumpers and the memory of my aunt's attempts to keep her nieces trendy still give me nightmares! Hipness is usually an intangible: if you describe something as 'hip', then the cachet, the rightness of it, is somehow immediately lost. It lingers around for a while, of course, so that someone makes money from the item, the image, the followers, but once the declaration has been made, those who seek hipness have already started to move on. This is rather depressing for those of us who spend our days designing objects in an effort to produce interesting and original items, so I decided to think a little more.

Perhaps hipness is really a reflection of a series of small changes that cumulatively bring about a much bigger change in attitude. Good design is always 'hip' because it does not depend on the whims of fashion to make us appreciate it. Think of an Eames chair or a perfectly cut Chanel suit.

With this in mind, I set out to produce a set of simple, tasteful designs that take a modern approach to hand knitting and use colour and yarn texture to make them covetable 'objects of desire'. The patterns are designed to be easy to follow, whether or not you've knitted before, and to give a taste of the amazing number of possibilities that can be achieved with very simple equipment. I hope they encourage you to develop your own ideas and become an experimental knitter.

In terms of quality, today's knitters probably have access to some of the finest yarns that have ever been available to the general public. Over the past 20 years, however, the choice of yarns has become a lot more limited, mainly because we are no longer knitting our own everyday garments. This sometimes means that we need to be inventive and make up our own yarns for projects. For example, you might choose to work two strands of double-knitting yarn together in a colour you really like to obtain the effect of a chunky yarn, or add a very fine strand of a mohair or cotton yarn to a thicker plain one in order to get more variety. Mixing your own yarns might appear a daunting prospect, but once you've found a mix you like and have decided on a needle size that gives the right tension and texture, you are well on the way to designing your own experimental, 'hip' pieces. A number of the projects in this book use mixtures of yarn and will hopefully inspire you to try this method. Have fun!

Getting Started

Equipment

Using and Choosing Knitting Yarn

When following a pattern or creating your own colourway, always check each yarn label to ensure that you are purchasing balls from the same dye lot – this avoids slight colour variations in the completed work. In addition, aim to buy enough yarn to complete the project so that on returning to the store to bolster your stocks you don't discover that the dye lot has been sold and the next batch, even though technically the same shade, is a marginally different colour. The manufacturers take every precaution to get the colours to match, but it's best to avoid even subtle variations.

If you decide to substitute a yarn for the one that has been recommended it is advisable to examine them together to check that they are close in weight, that they feel the same and that they stretch in a similar way. If the elasticity of the yarn is different, the finished article may not spring back into shape in the same way once it has been stretched.

Types of Knitting Needle

There are essentially three types of knitting needle: single-pointed, double-pointed and circular. Single-pointed needles can be used for most projects, whereas double-pointed needles are used only for items made up in tubular form such as socks. Circular needles usually have metal tips joined by a thin length of plastic cord. They are used to knit round seamless items, but should be at least 5cm (2in) less in length than the circumference of the finished project.

Single-pointed and double-pointed needles are made in aluminium, plastic and bamboo and which of these types you choose is entirely personal. Charity shops can be a good source if you just want to try your hand at knitting without investing in new needles. If you're keen to knit quickly, stitches seem to slide more easily on metal needles and you can really speed things up by wiping the needles with a soft cloth and a multi-surface cleaning polish, especially one that contains silicone. The length of needle you choose depends on the width of the project under construction and whether or not you like to knit with one needle tucked under your arm.

NEEDLE SIZES

In Europe and the UK the needle diameter is measured in millimetres. This means that the higher the number, the thicker the needle and the bigger the stitch. In Britain there are still many pairs of needles to be found with sizes based on the old British system. How this system compares to metric and American sizes is shown in the table below. Each project also specifies these three sizes.

Metric sizes (mm)	US sizes	UK/Canadian	Metric sizes (mm)	US sizes	UK/Canadian
2.0	0	14	6.0	10	4
2.25	1	13	6.5	10½	3
2.75	2	12	7.0	-	2
3.0	-	11	7.5	-	1
3.25	3	10	8.0	11	0
3.5	4	-	9.0	13	00
3.75	5	9	10.0	15	000
4.0	6	8	12.0	17	-
4.5	7	7	16.0	19	-
5.0	8	6	19.0	35	-
5.5	9	5	25.0	50	-

Accessories

Various simple accessories are available to help when knitting and making up. A stitch holder (available in various sizes) keeps stitches safe, for example on one side of a sock when the stitches on the other side are being worked. Colourful glass-headed pins are best for pinning pattern pieces together as they don't get lost among the fibres, and large-eyed tapestry or 'knitters' needles are essential for threading yarns for sewing up seams. These, along with a sharp pair of scissors, are all you will need to make up the patterns in this book.

Techniques

CASTING ON — TWO-NEEDLE METHOD

There are many methods of casting on and each knitter tends to have their own favourite. This one is suggested for most of the projects in this book because it gives a firm, elastic edge and is ideal for the featured pieces. The two-needle method makes it easy to form a tidy, moderately loose cast-on row with two needles. It really is worth while to practise until you feel confident that you can produce a cast-on that is going to look good and be comfortable to work from. If you are a complete beginner, read through the instructions for working knit stitch shown on pages 14–15 before going through the following instructions.

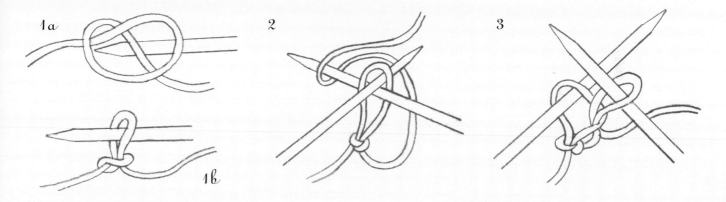

1. Form a slip knot for the first stitch by making a loop about 15cm (6in) from the yarn end and pull the short end through with the point of your knitting needle. Tighten the loop on to the needle.
2. Hold the needle with the slip knot in your left hand and take the yarn round it in the same way as for knitting.
3. Draw the yarn through to make a new stitch but instead of dropping the first loop from the left needle, keep it on the needle and then transfer the new stitch to the left needle.

TIP After the first two stitches have been formed, you can continue in this way until you have made the number of stitches required – however, this gives quite a tight row of stitches. To avoid this you can insert the needle between the first two stitches instead of into the first stitch on the left-hand needle. This simple change makes the first row much easier to work from.

KNIT – UK HOLD

The knit stitch is one of the two stitches that are basic to all knitting projects. The stitches are worked from the left-hand needle on to the right with the yarn controlled by the index finger of the right hand. There are other ways to wrap the yarn, and as you practise you will probably find a style that will suit you and help you to produce even stitches.

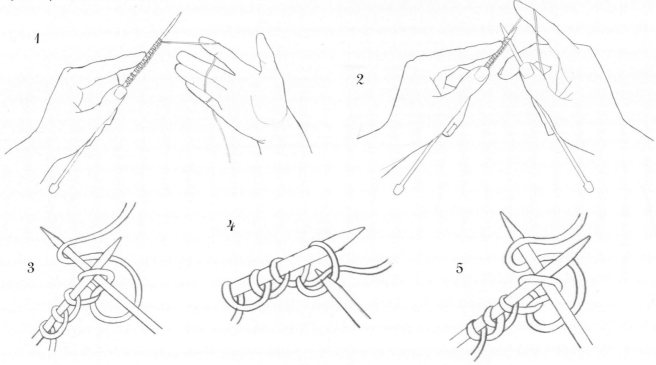

1. The needle with the cast-on stitches is held in the left hand with the first stitch close to the needle point. The yarn is wrapped round the fingers of your right hand with about 5cm (2in) of yarn between the first stitch and your index finger.
2. Having mastered the basic hold, insert the right needle into the front of the first stitch (from right to left) and recheck that the yarn is positioned correctly in the right hand.
3. The right index finger brings the yarn under the right needle and then back in between the crossed needles.
4. The loop on the right needle is drawn towards you and through the first stitch. At the same time, the first stitch on the left-hand needle is pushed towards the needle point and allowed to slip off.
5. The new stitch stays on the right needle. As you knit along each row, use your left thumb, index and middle fingers to push along the stitches towards the needle point of the left-hand needle. Use your right thumb to slide the stitches backwards along the right-hand needle.

KNIT – CONTINENTAL HOLD

The key to developing speed is to hold the needles lightly and keep your movements to a minimum. Speed is probably best achieved using this method of knitting where yarn is transferred from the left index finger rather than the right, involving wrist rather than finger movements. Try both methods to discover the one that suits you best.

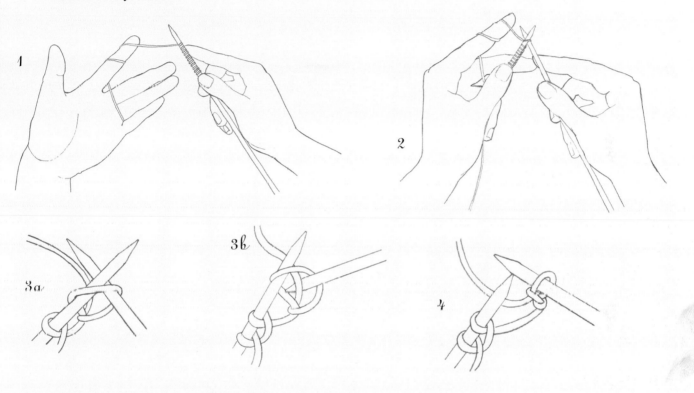

1. The needle with the cast-on stitches is held in the right hand and the yarn is wrapped round the left hand. The yarn should extend about 5cm (2in) from the first stitch.
2. The needle with stitches is transferred to the left hand and the yarn is pulled behind the needle. The first stitch is pushed up towards the needle point and the right needle inserted into the front (from right to left).
3. The tip of the right needle is twisted towards you and used to pull a loop of yarn through the stitch.
4. At the same time, the first stitch on the left-hand needle is pushed towards the needle point and allowed to slip off. The new stitch remains on the right-hand needle. As you knit along each row, use your left thumb and middle finger to push along the stitches towards the needle point of the left-hand needle. Use your right thumb to slide the stitches backwards along the right-hand needle.

PURL – UK HOLD

A purl stitch is a knit stitch worked in reverse. This is why the stitches all look the same when a garment is worked in stocking stitch (one row of knit followed by one row of purl). However, purl stitches do tend to be looser because fractionally more yarn is used per stitch. With practice, purl and knit stitches tend to even out and most knitters do not notice any tension differences in their work.

   With the UK hold, the needle with the cast-on stitches is held in the left hand and the yarn wrapped round the right hand in the same way as for the knit stitch. At the beginning the yarn is held at the front of the work and the right-hand needle enters the front of the first stitch.

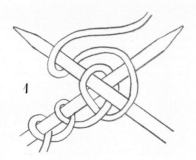

1. The right-hand needle points upwards slightly as it is inserted in the front of the stitch from right to left. The yarn is then taken backwards over the needles, and then back towards you under the right needle.
2. A loop is formed that is pulled through the first left-hand needle stitch. At the same time, the first left-hand needle stitch is pushed towards the needle tip.
3. The first stitch is slipped off the left-hand needle and the new stitch remains on the right-hand needle. The stitches are moved along the needles as the row is continued in the same way as the knit stitch.

PURL – CONTINENTAL HOLD

In this version of the purl stitch, the needle with the cast-on stitches is held in the left hand and the yarn is wrapped round the right hand in just the same way as the knit stitch. At the beginning, the needle with the stitches is transferred to the left hand and the index finger is extended to pull the yarn in front of the needle.

1. The right-hand needle points upwards slightly as it is inserted in the front of the stitch.
2. The left wrist is turned so that the yarn on the index finger comes towards you. You then push back and down with the right needle to draw a loop back through the stitch. At the same time, the stitch on the left needle should be pushed towards the tip.
3. The first stitch on the left-hand needle is slipped off the needle and the index finger is straightened to tighten the new stitch on the right needle. The stitches are moved along the needles as the row is continued in the same way as the knit stitch.

TIP Using this method, changing the yarn from knit to purl position can be speeded up by keeping the index finger close to the work and then working the stitches close to the needle tips.

TENSION SWATCHES

The only means of ensuring that knitting can be copied accurately is to specify the tension of a piece of knitting when worked using a particular yarn and needle size. The tension is the number of stitches and rows that were obtained per centimetre or inch of knitting. For greater accuracy, the stitches and rows are usually measured over a distance of 10cm (4in).

Before starting work with a new pattern, check the tension by working a sample, which should be slightly larger than a 10cm (4in) square. Place the sample right side up on a flat surface, pin the corners without stretching it and measure it against a tape measure. It can be helpful to put two pins 10cm (4in) apart to use as reference points when counting.

If you knit the sample and count more stitches and rows than are specified, knit another sample using a needle that is a size larger. If you count fewer stitches, knit another sample using a needle that is a size smaller. It is more crucial to get the number of stitches, rather than rows, right, as the number of rows can always be altered by knitting one or two rows more or less.

INCREASING

Increasing in knitting means adding stitches to a piece in addition to those that were originally cast on. At the beginning (or end) of a row, unless the knitting instructions state otherwise, the simplest method is usually to work a cast-on stitch and then knit or purl into the loop remaining on the left-hand needle, rather than letting it slip off. This is sometimes given as 'knit (or purl) twice into the first (or last) next stitch' in knitting instructions.

You can also increase by wrapping the yarn round the needle more than once, but this method leaves a hole in the knitting and is therefore a technique mostly used with lace patterns.

DECREASING

Decreasing the number of stitches will shape your work by making it narrower. There are various advanced methods of decreasing, such as when shaping a V-neck jumper, but for simple decreasing at the edges of a piece the 'knit (or purl) 2 together' method is all that is required.

TIP Another simple decreasing method is to cast off one stitch, as described in the casting-off section, but this is usually used when several stitches need to be cast off, such as when starting to shape an armhole.

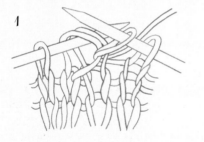

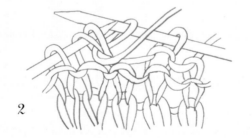

1. Decreasing in knitting involves knitting together through the first (or next) 2 stitches on the left-hand needle.
2. Decreasing in purl works by purling together through the first (or next) 2 stitches on the left-hand needle.

PLAIN CASTING OFF

This is the simplest method of removing stitches from a needle in a way that prevents them from coming undone. It is usually carried out with the knit side of the work facing you, but if you are casting off a rib it is usual to keep up the knit/purl sequence you have been using rather than casting off all the stitches in knit. In this instance the instruction 'cast off in rib' would be used rather than the more standard 'cast off'.

TIP If you tend to knit very tightly, it can be a good idea to cast off using a right-hand needle that is one size larger than the left. Another tip is to use a thicker yarn for casting off, which will give a neater edge – this method is demonstrated in the Wool-Slub cushion on page 90.

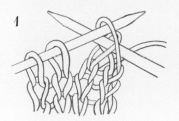
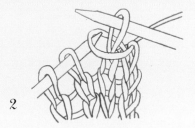

1. The first 2 stitches of the row are worked and the yarn is held taut at the back. The first worked stitch is passed over the second, using the left-hand needle.
2. This leaves a single stitch on the right-hand needle.

NEATENING ENDS

All loose ends of yarn are usually woven into the side seams of a knitted piece before the work is ironed and the seams are sewn together. Each loose end is threaded on to a large-eye tapestry needle (these are often sold as 'knitters needles') and woven in either down the side seam, or occasionally along the row on the reverse side. About 5cm (2in) would be the correct length of yarn to sew in, but this varies with the thickness of the yarn.

FINISHING USING A STEAM IRON

When working with natural fibre yarns – such as 100 per cent merino wools, silk and pure cotton – a steam iron should be used at the wool or cotton setting, as appropriate, to give a professional finish to the finished pieces. Steam restores moisture and relaxes the fibres, allowing them to be 'set' into shape by the heat of the iron. If you need to increase the size or alter the shape of a natural fibre fabric piece, it is possible to pin the piece to a padded ironing board to the required shape and then steam it with an iron. After steaming, it is important to leave the fabric to dry thoroughly to ensure that the required finish is maintained.

Synthetic yarns do not respond so well to heat, so always closely follow the manufacturer's instructions on the yarn label.

TIP Within a knitting pattern, a set of stitches which is to be repeated is usually shown by an asterisk (*) at the beginning and end of the instruction. The pattern will also give an instruction for when you should stop working the * to * repeats.

If more than one type of repeat of stitches is used in the same pattern the second set of instructions will be enclosed by different symbols e.g. two asterisks (** to **).

Types of Knit

GARTER STITCH

This, the simplest of all stitch patterns, is the name given to the pattern produced when every row is knitted. The same effect is achieved by purling every row – the use of purling in this way is referred to as 'reverse garter stitch'.

STOCKING STITCH

Stocking stitch is knitted by working one row in knit and purling the following row. It produces a fabric that is smooth on one side (the knitted side) and tightly looped on the reverse (the purl side). T-shirt fabric, tights and 1980s leggings are all commercial examples of stocking stitch. The knit side is usually considered to be the 'right' side but sometimes the purl side is used for the main side – then the pattern is referred to as 'reverse stocking stitch'.

RIBBED KNIT

Rib patterns create a series of vertical ridges in a fabric. They are produced when units of knit and purl stitches are alternated along one row. On the following row knit stitches are purled and purl stitches are knitted. The ratio of knit to purl may be even, for example in 1 x 1, 2 x 2 and 3 x 3 ribs that all involve alternating equal numbers of knit and purl stitches (see below), or it may be uneven (see top of page 21). Sometimes an extra stitch, or unit of stitches, is added to the end of a rib to give symmetrical balance – this would be required, for example, when knitting the welt of a jumper. Ribbed fabrics are much looser and more elastic if worked on the same-size needles as those used for stocking or garter stitch with the same yarn. For this reason, smaller-sized needles than those given on the yarn label are usually used for rib.

UNEVEN RIBBED KNIT

An uneven rib is made up of wider knit ridges that are interspersed with single purl stitches, for example in 2 x 1, 3 x 1, or 4 x 1 ribs. On the following row the stitches are reversed. An uneven rib creates a less elastic fabric, demonstrated in the Wide-Rib Table Runner on page 48, which uses a 5 x 1 rib to give texture. A more elastic rib would be inappropriate to use here.

STRIPED KNITTING

Stripes come in all widths and colours. The benefit of knitted stripes is that simple stitches can be used in combination with the full creative potential of colour combinations. Many patterns in plain stocking stitch can be reworked creatively with stripes, provided the yarns chosen can be knitted to the same tension as those specified by the pattern. Some plain and blended yarns seem destined to be used together, such as the new cotton yarns used in the Granny's Shopper on page 66.

Fine lurex thread can be knitted along with a plain yarn for stripes with added sparkle, or alternatively just insert one line of a really bright colour as a highlight among neutrals – this is demonstrated in the Striped Chunky Throw on page 42.

EMBELLISHED KNITTING

In the same way that stripes add interest to simple stitches it is possible to enhance a finished knitted piece with embroidery by using cross stitch or working duplicate stitches over the knitting. There is nothing to stop you using knitted fabric as a base for whatever design takes your fancy, but don't get too carried away and remember that simple is generally best.

Another method of embellishing is to use beads and sequins that are threaded on to the yarn before it is knitted. This is a simple but effective way to create a unique and luxurious effect. The Spider's-Web Evening Scarf on page 72 demonstrates this technique.

TEXTURED KNITTING

The simplest way to create texture is to work in familiar stitches using a textured yarn, as shown in the Wool-Slub Cushion on page 90. Another idea is to combine textures by learning some new stitches, such as those suggested for the Panelled Baby Blanket on page 82.

Stocking Stitch

Fingerless Mitts

Fingerless gloves, a style first made popular in the 1950s, have remained a familiar fashion accessory, carrying a classic appeal that never seems to wane. Maybe this is because they are incredibly practical as well as fun to wear. These fingerless mitts are easy to make – avoiding the complications of working the full finger shapes of each hand!

PATTERN
Basic hand structure
• Cast on 50 stitches in the main yarn using the two-needle method.
• Work 10cm (4in) in stocking stitch (knit one row, purl one row) commencing with a knit row. Take the measurement from the cast-on edge, even though the edge will roll as you work.
• Commence shaping one side of the mitt by working the first 25 stitches of the next knit row before turning the work to purl back along the stitches. The 25 stitches that will be used to knit the other side of the mitt can remain on the needle while you work the first side. Continue in stocking stitch until the first side measures 16cm (6½in) from the cast-on edge. Break off the yarn and rejoin it in order to work the second side to match in length. Both sides should be on the same needle when they are the same length. Break off the yarn.

Contrast edging
• Rejoin the trim yarn and work 2.5cm (1in) of stocking stitch first on one side and then on the other before casting off. See 1

Thumb finger
• Now place the work with the right side facing you and pick up stitches for the thumb. To pick up a stitch, work in knit and transfer the made stitch from the right-hand needle back on to the left-hand needle before picking up the next stitch.

• Pick up the 9 stitches from the left side of the divide (i.e. each end stitch from 9 rows above the point where the 2 sides split).
• Make 1 stitch from the yarn loops at the divide, working up 1 stitch from several loose strands if necessary. See 2
• Then pick up 9 stitches from the row ends on the opposite side in the same way. There should be 19 stitches in total on your left-hand needle. Work 2cm (¾in) in stocking stitch and then change yarn to create 2.5cm (1in) of contrast trim. This will naturally roll. See 3

TO MAKE UP
• Press lightly with a steam iron on a flat surface and leave to dry. Avoid forcing the fabric too flat because the rolling edges are a feature of the design – this is done by not pinning the cast-on and off edges down before pressing.
• Sew the side and thumb seams of the main colour with the right sides of the work facing, but remember to allow the wrist and contrast edges to roll so that these are sewn on the inside to give a neat finish.
• Put in a couple of oversew stitches to secure the rolled edge at either side on the contrast trim. Sew any loose ends of yarn into the seams.

YARN
Main: 1 x 50g (1¾oz) ball Jaeger Matchmaker Merino 4-ply, shade 639 Granite

Trim: 1 x 50g (1¾oz) ball Jaeger Baby Merino 4-ply, shade 096 Marigold

NEEDLES
1 pair 3.25mm/UK 10/US 3 needles

TENSION
Working with 3.25mm/UK 10/US 3 needles, 36 rows x 28 stitches make a 10cm (4in) square

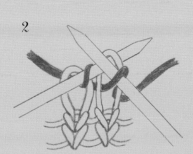

Cube Footstool

Have fun making this cube footstool as a funky accessory. The one shown opposite is a combination of neutral browns and creams spiced up with a taste of hot pink, but you can select colours to suit the room's purpose: primary colours for a child's room, tweed effects for a country style, sleek neutrals for an urban look or fur effects to add character and warmth. With the diverse range of chunky yarns that are available, this project allows you to stamp the personality of your choice on your home.

PATTERN

- It is important to check your tension to ensure a good fit.
- For colours A, B, D and E, knit 40cm height x 45cm width (15¾in height x 17¾in width) sections, as follows:
  - A: 56 rows x 50 stitches
  - B and E: 80 rows x 68 stitches
  - D: 56 rows x 50 stitches
- For colours C and F knit 45 x 45cm (17¾ x 17¾in) sections, as follows:
  - C: 63 rows x 50 stitches
  - F: 90 rows x 68 stitches

TO MAKE UP

- Gently press out the sections using a steam iron.
- Then lay the sections out so that you can work out their placement on the cube. Starting with the top section C, pin sections A, B, D and E to it so that the edges meet with the wrong sides together. See 1
- Sew up all the sides on the machine using a 0.5cm (⅛in) seam allowance, joining 5 sides of the cube and leaving 1 side open.
- Press the seams, turn the right way out and insert the foam block. See 2
- Lay the last section F on to the cube, fold the hems under and pin into place. Carefully handsew to secure. See 3

TIP Correct any minor differences in size either by using the steam iron to stretch a section (if you are using a pure wool yarn) or by adjusting the seam allowance, avoiding bulky seams wherever possible.

YARN

A: 2 x 100g (3½oz) balls Rowan Big Wool, shade 030 Tricky

B: 4 x 50g (1¾oz) balls Jaeger Extra Fine Merino Chunky, shade 25 Toast

C: 2 x 100g (3½oz) balls Rowan Plaid, shade 166 Driftwood

D: 2 x 100g (3½oz) balls Rowan Plaid, shade 165 Washed Pebble

E: 4 x 50g (1¾oz) balls Jaeger Extra Fine Merino Chunky, shade 22 Loam

F: 2 x 100g (3½oz) hanks Rowan Spun Chunky 981, shade Pebble

NEEDLES

A: 1 pair 9mm/UK 00/US 13 needles

B and E: 1 pair 6mm/UK 4/ US 10 needles

C and D: 1 pair 8mm /UK 0/ US 11 needles

F: 1 pair 7–8mm/UK 2–0/ US 10.5–11 needles

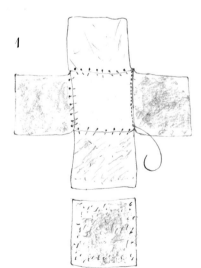

1

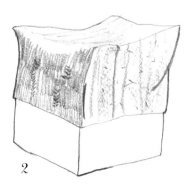

2

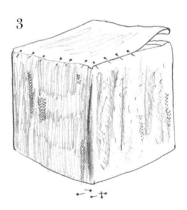

3

TENSION

A: 14 rows x 11 stitches make a 10cm (4in) square

B and E: 20 rows x 15 stitches make a 10cm (4in) square

C and D: 14–16 rows x 11–12 stitches make a 10cm (4in) square

F: 16–17 rows x 12–13 stitches make a 10cm (4in) square

ADDITIONAL MATERIALS

Upholstery foam, the denser the better (available from upholstery suppliers), cut to 40cm height x 45cm width x 45cm depth (15¾in height x 17¾in width x 17¾in depth)

Sewing machine

Polycotton thread to match yarn

Sewing needle

Pins

Cosy Aran Bedsocks

Always wanted to try knitting socks but afraid to try four needles and complicated shaping? These have a simple fitted style that can be altered according to your shoe size. We used an Aran yarn that is easy to control when you're learning a new technique, knits up satisfyingly quickly and feels great. In circular knitting a stocking-stitch effect is produced without using purl stitches. Once you've tried it, you'll be desperate to find more patterns that will allow you to work with cylinders of fabric.

PATTERN

Leg

• In the trim yarn cast on 42 [46] stitches using the two-needle method and then transfer approximately one-third of the stitches to each of the double-pointed needles. See 1 The extra needle is used to knit each stitch as you go round.

• Knit 3 rounds in the trim yarn, working the stitches tightly to make a neat join where the first and second rounds meet.

• Change to the main yarn and continue until your tube measures 20cm (8in) [22cm (8½in)] from the cast-on edge.

Heel

• Transfer 21 [23] of the stitches to a stitch holder. See 2

• Change to working with the pair of 4mm/UK 8/US 6 needles and decrease 1 stitch at both ends of every following row until 11 [13] stitches remain. Remember that you will now need to purl on the reverse side rows.

• Work 2 rows and then increase 1 stitch at both ends of every following row until you have 21 [23] stitches again. See 3

Foot

• Arrange the heel stitches, plus those from the stitch holder, back on to 3 double-pointed needles, once again using 14 on each needle, and recommence circular knitting for 10cm (4in) [14cm (5½in)] from the heel split. See 4

Toe

• Divide the stitches so that 21 [23] will form the base of the toe and 21 [23] the top of the toe. The top 21 [23] stitches are transferred to a stitch holder. Using 2 needles and stocking stitch, decrease 1 stitch at both ends of every following row until 11 [13] remain. Work 4 rows and then increase 1 stitch at both ends of every following row until you have 21 [23] stitches again. See 5

Toe seam

• Transfer the stitch-holder stitches to the spare needle and arrange them so that they are held behind the 21 [23] toe stitches, ready to be cast off together in knit. Slip the first stitch from the back needle in front of the first stitch of the front needle and knit them together. Repeat for the second stitches and then pass the first stitch on the right-hand needle over the second (in other words a normal cast-off). Repeat until all stitches are cast off. See 6 and 7

• Work the second sock in the same way.

TO MAKE UP

Steam-iron the pieces to shape before sewing up the heel seams and sewing in any loose ends into the seams.

YARN

Trim: 1 x 50g (1¾oz) ball Jaeger Extra Fine Merino Aran, shade 551 Pandora

Body: 2 x 50g (1¾oz) balls Jaeger Extra Fine Merino Aran, shade 539 Honesty

NEEDLES

1 set of 4 double-pointed needles size 4mm/UK 8/US 6

1 pair 4mm/UK 8/US 6 needles

1 extra single-pointed needle, size 3.25mm/UK 10/US 3 (or smaller)

TENSION

Working in stocking stitch with 4mm/UK 8/US 6 needles, 25 rows x 19 stitches make a 10cm (4in) square

ADDITIONAL MATERIALS

Large-eye needle for sewing up

Stitch holder (or large safety pin)

SIZE

To fit shoe size 3–5 UK (5–7.5 US) [size 6–7 UK (8–9.5 US)]

(size 3–5 given first with size 6–7 in square brackets)

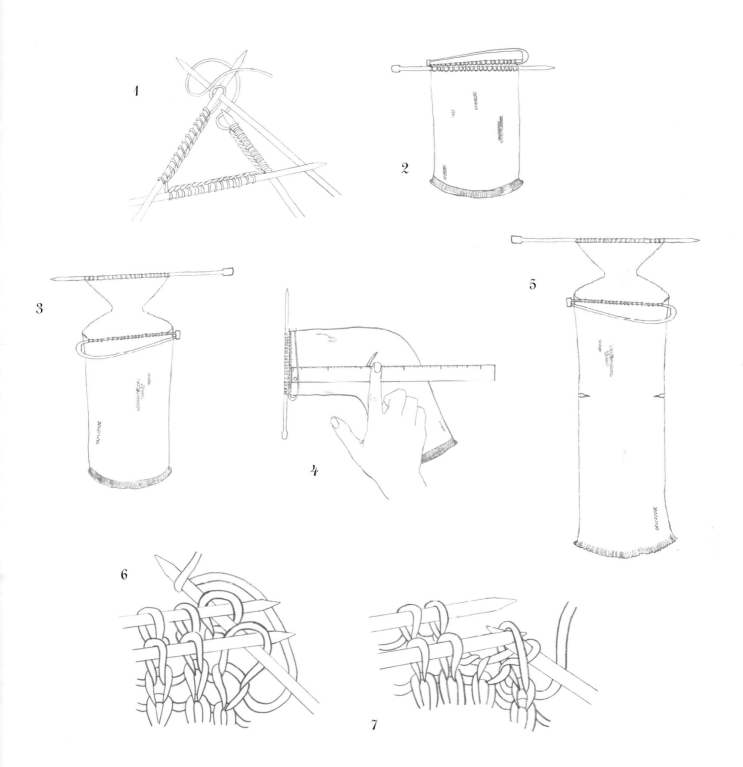

Garter Stitch

Hotwater-Bottle Cover

Hotwater-bottle covers come in all shapes and sizes these days. I have certainly designed a fair number of these comforting 'objects of desire' in response to their unceasing popularity. The softness and sophistication of a pure wool yarn and a slightly retro pattern give this design that all-important cuddle factor that never goes out of fashion.

PATTERN

- Cast on 31 stitches using the two-needle method.
- Work 7 rows in stocking stitch commencing with a knit row (knit one row, purl one row and repeat for 7 rows).
- Row 8: knit – this is the start of the garter-stitch pattern.
- Rows 9–25: knit.
- Row 26: purl.
- Rows 27–57: purl.
- Row 58: purl.
- Row 59: knit.
- Row 60: purl.
- Rows 61–73: knit.
- Row 74: purl.
- Row 75: knit.
- Row 76: purl.
- Row 77–100: knit.
- Row 101: purl.
- Rows 102 and 103: knit.
- Commence the shaping for the neck of the hotwater-bottle by casting off 7 stitches at the beginning of the next 2 rows (both are knit rows). See 1
- Decrease 1 stitch at the beginning of the next 2 rows – simply knit 2 stitches together to decrease neatly at the beginning of the row and continue in knit.
- The shaping continues in knit, unless a purl row is specified, as follows:
  - Knit 2 rows.
  - Increase 1 stitch at the beginning of the next 2 rows – knit into the front and back of the first stitch to increase.
  - Knit 12 rows.
  - Decrease 1 stitch at the beginning of the next 2 rows.
  - Purl 1 row.
  - Knit 1 row.
  - Decrease 1 stitch at the beginning of the next 2 rows (both knit).
  - Make 7 new stitches at the beginning of the next 2 rows (both knit).
  - Knit 9 rows. See 2
- Cast off in knit or make a loop to fasten the cover with a button loop, as follows:
- Cast off 15 stitches, then wind the yarn round the right-hand needle and pass it through the cast-off loop. Repeat 5 times. See 3
- Knit the next 2 stitches on the left-hand needle together so that you pass them through the cast-off loop and make a neat finish on the button loop. Complete the cast-off to the end of the row.

TO MAKE UP

- Steam-iron lightly on a flat surface and leave to dry.
- Pin and sew the side seams of the body of the hotwater-bottle cover with the right sides of the work facing. Sew the top and neck together, again with right sides facing.
- Sew the side seam of the top front on to the body before reversing the top and neck. Sew in any loose ends of yarn.

YARN

2 x 100g (3½oz) balls Rowan Polar wool, shade 650 Smirk

NEEDLES

1 pair 7.5mm/UK 1/US 11 needles

TENSION

14 rows x 11 stitches make a 10cm (4in) square

ADDITIONAL MATERIALS

Large-eye needle for sewing up

Button

Pins

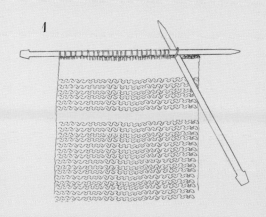

1

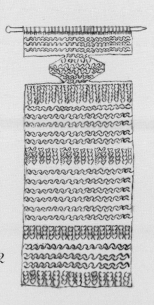

2

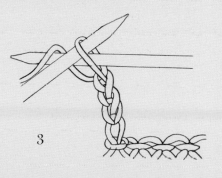

3

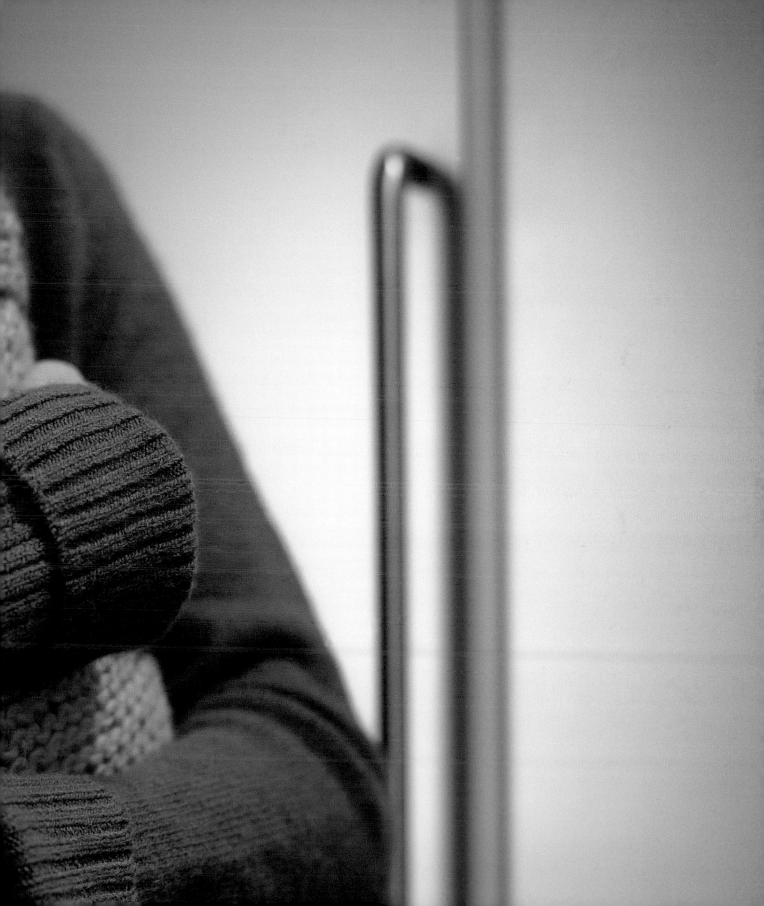

Luxury Lavender Pillow

A neck pillow is always welcome for those moments when you need to sit back and relax, particularly when travelling. The cover for this one is knitted in wool with a pretty basket stitch, but you could easily make it in 4-ply cotton yarn. You will need to make a fabric pillow and choose your favourite filling. A wide variety of suitable fillings are available from craft shops and herbalists – a mixture of heat-treated buckwheat, dried camomile and dried lavender is my favourite.

PATTERN

• Cast on 47 stitches using the two-needle method and work 16.5cm (6½in) in stocking stitch.
• Change to 'basket stitch' on a knit row as follows:
• Row 1: knit 1 *(purl 3, knit 3)*. Repeat from * to * to final 4 stitches, purl 3, knit 1.
• Row 2: purl 1 **(knit 3, purl 3)**. Repeat from ** to ** to final 4 stitches, knit 3, purl 1.
• Row 3: as row 1.
• Row 4: as row 1.
• Row 5: as row 2.
• Row 6: as row 1.
• Repeat these 6 rows 19 times, then work rows 1–3. This should give a pattern of 41-row blocks.
• On the next row purl across the row – this marks the return to stocking stitch.
• Continue in stocking stitch for 18cm (7¼in). Cast off in purl. *See 1*

TO MAKE UP

• Make up a fabric pillow to the length and width of the basket-stitch middle section. Using a spare length of fabric, cut out a rectangle twice the length of, and slightly wider than, the basket-stitch section. Fold the strip in half with right sides facing and then machine sew the raw edges. Leave a gap of about 4cm (1½in) in one of the seams so that you can pour in the filling when you turn the bag inside out.
• Use the funnel to pour in the filling until the bag is about three-quarters full. *See 2* Turn the raw edges to the inside and machine-sew across the opening.
• Press the knitted cover lightly with a steam iron on a flat surface, allowing the cast-on and cast-off edges to roll slightly.
• With the right sides of the pillow facing inwards, fold the shorter-side flap into the centre of the middle section. Then sew up the side seams using yarn and a large-eye needle. When you reach the middle section, stretch the edges of the flap outwards using the elasticity of the knitting to ensure a snug fit for the pillow.
• Fold in the other flap, which should overlap the section you have already sewn by a few centimetres. Pin and handsew the side seams, again making sure that you stretch out the sides of the cast-off edge. *See 3*
• The slightly bulky seams will disappear when you turn the cover right side out and insert the pillow. *See 4*

YARN

1 x 50g (1¾oz) ball Jaeger Matchmaker Merino 4-ply wool, shade SH747 Bloom

NEEDLES

1 pair 3.75mm/UK 9 /US 5 needles

TENSION

31 rows x 26 stitches make a 10cm (4in) square

ADDITIONAL MATERIALS

Length of linen or cotton fabric to make an inner pillow

Suitable filling; here a mixture of buckwheat, dried camomile and lavender was used

Kitchen funnel or cut-off end of a small plastic mineral-water bottle

Sewing machine

Thread to match yarn

Large-eye needle for sewing up

Sewing needle

Pins

Striped Chunky Throw

This unfussy contemporary throw is perfect for accessorizing the end of a bed or a sofa. Stripes of plain and blended chunky yarns are linked using bright highlights and an interesting random texture is created using stocking stitch, garter and reverse garter stitch.

PATTERN

- Rewind one of the yarn B balls into 2 balls, so that you have 3 balls from which to create 3 strands for knitting. See 1
- Cast on 60 stitches using yarn A and work 4 rows in stocking stitch (a knit row followed by a purl row).
- Continue in garter stitch (all rows knit) for 30cm (12in).
- With the right side facing and using 3 strands of yarn B worked together, knit 1 row. See 2
- Change to yarn C and reverse garter stitch (all rows purl) for 20cm (8in) followed by 5cm (2in) in stocking stitch.
- With the right side facing, change to yarn D and work 15cm (6in) in garter stitch.
- Again with the right side facing, change to 2 strands of yarn E worked together and work 30cm (12in) in garter stitch.
- With the reverse side facing, purl 1 row using 2 strands of yarn F worked together.
- Change to 3 strands of yarn G and garter stitch for 5cm (2in) followed by 2cm (¾in) of stocking stitch.
- Change to yarn C and continue in garter stitch for 15cm (6in).
- Do not break off the yarn, but change to yarn B and, using 3 strands worked together, work 1 row before continuing with yarn C in stocking stitch for 9cm (3½in).

- Change to yarn A, continue with stocking stitch for 5cm (2in) and then garter stitch for 10cm (4in).
- Insert 2 rows of yarn C in stocking stitch, and another 6cm (2½in) of garter stitch using yarn A and then add another 2 rows of yarn C in stocking stitch.
- Change to 2 strands of yarn E worked together and then knit 17cm (7in) of garter stitch.
- Insert one row using 3 strands of yarn B worked together before continuing in garter stitch using yarn C for 5cm (2in).
- Insert 1 row using 2 strands of yarn E worked together before continuing in garter stitch using yarn A for 10cm (4in).
- Insert 2 rows of yarn C, still in garter stitch, before working the final 12cm (4¾in) in garter stitch using yarn H.
- To finish the throw, continue in yarn H and use stocking stitch for approximately 4cm (1½in), so that you can then cast off in knit.

TO MAKE UP

Sew in the loose ends of yarn on the reverse side of the throw. Do this by weaving the threaded sewing needle through the backs of the knitted stitches for about 10cm (4in), working across the row of matching yarn. See 3

YARNS (in order of first use)

A: 9 x 100g (3½oz) balls Rowan Biggy Print, shade SH258 Sheep

B: 2 x 50g (1¾oz) balls Rowan Cotton Tape, shade SH543 Shadow (rewind the ball into 2 approximately equal balls)

C: 7 x 100g (3½oz) balls Rowan Biggy Print, shade SH250 Swirl

D: 3 x 100g (3½oz) balls Rowan Biggy Print, shade SH244 Glum

E: 4 x 100g (3½oz) balls Rowan Plaid, shade SH163 Soft Kelp

F: 1 x 50g (1¾oz) ball Jaeger Extrafine Merino Aran, shade 551 Pandora (rewind the ball into 2 approximately equal balls)

G: 2 x 50g (1¾oz) balls Rowan Cotton Tape, shade SH544 Bamboo (rewind the ball into 2 approximately equal balls)

H: 2 x 100g (3½oz) balls Rowan Plaid, shade SH165 Washed Pebbles

NEEDLES

1 pair 12mm/UK 000/US 17 needles

Large-eye sewing needle/bodkin for sewing in loose ends of yarn

TENSION

Working in stocking stitch using Rowan Biggy Print and 12mm/ UK 000/US 17 needles, 10 rows x 7 stitches make a 10cm (4in) square

SIZE

200cm length x 90cm width (79in length x 35½in width)

Ribbed Knits

Wide-Rib Table Runner

This runner can be used to bring a flash of colour to a room or to coordinate with the rest of your dining accessories. The wide rib adds texture and the bands of narrower ribbing on the side edges ensure that the runner lies flat. The pattern can also be adapted to make tablemats, which look effective when worked in a solid colour or with matching bands of colour.

PATTERN

- Cast on 61 stitches using yarn B.
- Next row: (purl 1, knit 1) twice, *purl 5, knit 1* repeat from * to * to the last 3 stitches, (purl 1, knit 1, purl 1). See 1 (illustration shows reverse side of a 4 x 1 rib pattern.)
- Continue the rib pattern changing the yarn as indicated for the length of the runner, as follows:
  - Main yarn A: 14 rows.
  - Yarn C: 6 rows.
  - Main yarn A: 10 rows.
  - Yarn D: 2 rows.
  - Main yarn A: 6 rows.
  - Yarn C: 1 row.
  - Main yarn A: 30 rows.
  - Yarn D: 4 rows.
  - Main yarn A: 45 rows.
  - Yarn C: 1 row.
  - Main yarn A: 6 rows.
  - Yarn D: 2 rows.
  - Main yarn A: 10 rows.
  - Yarn C: 6 rows.
  - Main yarn A: 14 rows.
- The narrower 1 x 1 ribbing on the side edges helps the runner to lie flat. See 2
- Cast off the knitting in Yarn B, maintaining the rib pattern.
- To make tablemats in the same pattern, cast on 45 stitches and set up the same 5 x 1 rib using 1 x 1 rib edges and knit to a length of 30cm (12in).

TO MAKE UP

Press out the runner using a steam iron. See 3 Allow each section to cool before moving it – this will help the sides stay flat.

YARN

Main yarn A: 4 x 50g (1¾oz) balls Rowan Cotton Tape, shade 542 String

B: 1 x 50g (1¾oz) ball Rowan Cotton Tape, shade 543 Shadow

C: 1 x 50g (1¾oz) ball Rowan Cotton Tape, shade 555 Fever

D: 1 x 50g (1¾oz) ball Rowan Cotton Tape, shade 553 Acidic

NEEDLES

1 pair 6.5mm/UK 3/US 10½ needles

TENSION

Working in 5 x 1 rib, 26 rows x 15 stitches make a 10cm (4in) square

1
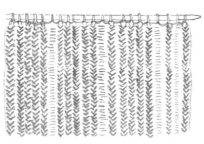

2

3
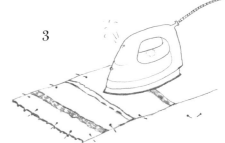

Ribbed Legwarmers

The trick with legwarmers is to leave the pastels of the 1980s behind! These are sized to fit an 'average' size 10/12 leg but they are easy to make wider or longer according to your requirements. The ribs are knitted here as different lengths, but you can easily adapt them to the desired measurements.

PATTERN

Ankle rib
• Starting with the shorter rib, cast on 84 stitches in the rib yarn with 2.75mm/UK 12/US 2 needles using the two-needle method.
• Work in knit 2, purl 2 rib for 8cm (3in) as follows:
Every row: *knit 2, purl 2* and repeat from * to * all along the row.

Leg section
• With the right side of the work facing you, change to 4.5mm/UK 7/US 7 needles and stripe-1 yarn and decrease the number of stitches worked as follows:
• Decrease row: (knit 2, purl 2 together) repeat to end (the decrease in stitches accommodates the thicker double-knitting yarn thickness). See 1
• Next row: purl.
• To complete the first stripe, work another 2 rows in stocking stitch (row 1: knit; row 2: purl). There is no need to break off the yarn as the next stripe is only 2 rows wide.
• Work another 2 rows in stocking stitch using stripe-2 yarn.
• The remaining stripes are worked without further shaping, repeating the sequence of

4 rows of stripe-1 yarn and 2 rows of stripe-2 yarn. Continue until the striped section is approximately 20cm (8in) long.
• However long you decide to make the finished item, end with a block of 4 rows of stripe-1 yarn.

Top rib
• To work the top rib, change to 2.75mm/UK 12/US 2 needles and the rib yarn. Increase the number of stitches worked on the first row as follows: (knit 1, knit twice into the next stitch, purl 2) to end.
• Continue to work in knit 2, purl 2, rib until the rib is 4cm (1½in) long. Cast off in rib.
• Work the second leg warmer in just the same way.

TO MAKE UP
• Steam-iron both pieces.
• Fold each so that the right sides are facing. See 2
• Pin and sew the side seams in back stitch with stripe-1 yarn. See 3
• Sew any short, unused lengths of yarn into the side seam. Finally, turn each legwarmer right side out.

YARN

Rib: 1 x 50g (1¾oz) ball Jaeger Alpaca 4-ply, shade 390 Crush

Stripe 1: 1 x 50g (1¾oz) ball Jaeger Matchmaker Merino Double Knitting, shade 888 Parma

Stripe 2: 1 x 50g (1¾oz) ball Jaeger Matchmaker Merino Double Knitting, shade 893 Flax

NEEDLES

1 pair 2.75mm/UK 12/US 2 needles

1 pair 4.5mm/UK 7/US 7 needles

TENSION

Using stripe-1 yarn and working in stocking stitch with 4.5mm/UK 7/US 7 needles, 28 rows x 20 stitches make a 10cm (4in) square

ADDITIONAL MATERIALS

Large-eye needle for sewing up

Pins

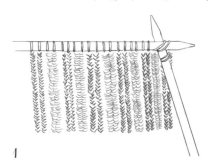

1

2

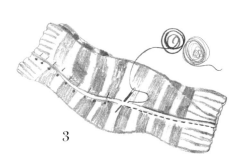

3

Garter-Stripe Tea & Egg Cosy

Keep your teapot and boiled eggs warm with this bright, mood-enhancing accessory for retro-style entertaining. These machine-washable cotton garter-stripe cosies are knitted in two pieces, starting off with a wide rib and continuing in garter stitch. Measure the height and circumference of your teapot before starting work to ensure that the cosy will be a snug fit.

PATTERN (TEA COSY)
Side 1 and side 2
Rib
• Cast on 47 stitches in the rib yarn on 4mm/UK 8/US 6 needles using the two-needle method and work 8 rows using the following wide rib pattern. Change to 5mm/UK 6/US 8 needles after the first row and continue using them for the rest of the pattern.
• Row 1: (knit 5, purl 2) repeat to last 5 stitches, knit 5.
• Row 2: (purl 5, knit 2) repeat to last 5 stitches, purl 5.
Stripes
• Change to stripe-1 yarn and work in garter stitch (all rows knit) for 10 rows.
• Change to stripe-2 yarn and work a further 10 rows garter stitch, followed by 4 rows in stripe-1 yarn.
• Commence shaping:
• Next row *knit 2 tog, knit 4*, repeat from * to * to last 5 stitches, knit 2 tog, knit 3.
• Knit 2 rows.
• Next row *knit 4, knit 2 tog*, repeat from * to *, knit the last 3 stitches.
• Knit 2 rows.
• Change to stripe-2 yarn and *knit 4, knit 2 tog*, knitting the remainder of the stitches at the end of the row. Knit the following row.

• Next row *knit 2 tog, knit 3* repeat from * to * to the last 4 stitches, knit 2, knit 2 tog.
• Next row knit.
• Repeat the previous two rows.
• *Knit 2 tog, knit 1*. Then repeat from * to * to the last 2 stitches, knit 2 tog. Leave about 30cm (12in) of yarn before breaking it off.
• Transfer the remaining stitches on to a stitch holder.

TO MAKE UP
• Steam-iron both pieces of the tea cosy and pin one side seam to the right sides facing. *See 1*
• Sew the rib and the first band together leaving a space (on the next 2 bands) for the teapot handle before then stitching the top band.
• On the other side sew the rib and the first band together, leave a space on the next band for the spout and then stitch the top band. Thread the cast-off yarn from one outside edge through all the stitches on the holders. Pull it tight and sew the thread into the side seam. *See 2* Sew up the other side to match. *See 3*
• Finally, trim the remaining short lengths of yarn from the stripes and sew the ends into the seams.

YARN
Rib: 1 x 50g (1¾oz) ball Jaeger Siena 4-ply, shade 424 Borage

Stripe 1: 1 x 50g (1¾oz) ball Jaeger Siena 4-ply, shade 426 Meadow

Stripe 2: 1 x 50g (1¾oz) ball Jaeger Siena 4-ply, shade 419 Cream

NEEDLES
1 pair 4mm/UK 8/US 6 needles
1 pair 5mm/UK 6/US 8 needles

TENSION
Working in garter stitch with 4mm/UK 8/US 6 needles, 30 rows x 19 stitches make a 10cm (4in) square

ADDITIONAL MATERIALS
Large-eye needle for sewing up
Stitch holder or a large safety pin
Pins

SIZE
17cm (7in) height x 25cm (10in) width and circumference approximately 50cm (20in)

You can make several egg cosies in the same yarn and design using any leftover yarn.

PATTERN (EGG COSY)
Side 1 and side 2
Rib
• Cast on 30 stitches on 4mm/UK 8/US 6 needles using the two-needle method and work 4 rows using the following wide rib pattern. Change to 5mm/UK 6/US 8 needles after the first row and then continue using these for the rest of the pattern.
• Row 1: (purl 2, knit 5) repeat to last 2 stitches, purl 2.
• Row 2: (knit 2, purl 5) repeat to last 2 stitches, knit 2.
Stripes
• Change to stripe-1 yarn and work in garter stitch (all rows knit) for 6 rows. Change to stripe-2 yarn and work a further row of garter stitch.

Commence shaping:
• Next row: *knit 3, knit 2 tog*, repeat from * to * to end.
• Next row: knit.
• Next row: knit 2 tog, repeat to end. Leave a 20cm (8in) length of cast-off yarn before breaking it off.
• Transfer the remaining stitches to a stitch holder.

TO MAKE UP
• Steam-iron both pieces, then pin and sew up one side seam with right sides facing.
• Thread the cast-off yarn from one outside edge through all the stitches on the holders. Pull tight and sew the thread into the side seam. Then sew up the other side.
• Trim the remaining short yarn lengths and sew them into the seams.

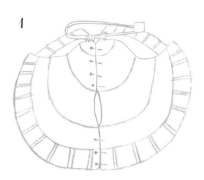
1

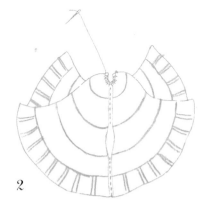
2

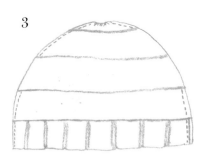
3

Striped Knits

Silk-and-Mohair Lampshade

With this project you can transform a simple lampshade into something special by means of a subtly striped cover. The varying densities of the silk and mohair yarns give the shade a very different look when the lamp is switched on. If you work through the calculations below, you can knit a perfectly fitted cover for any size shade.

CALCULATING THE PATTERN

Because your lampshade size is likely to be different from the one used here, you will need to work out the individual pattern for your lampshade cover.

• First measure the top circumference (a), height (b) and bottom circumference (c) of the shade. *See 1*

• Draw out a rectangle where the horizontal side length (a) is the top circumference measurement and the vertical side length (b) is the height.

• Work out the difference between the top and bottom circumferences (c − a), and extend the bottom line of the rectangle out by a quarter of this length on both sides (d). Then join the top and new bottom corners to give a trapezium-shape pattern. *See 2*

• Calculate the number of stitches to cast on for the bottom of the shade (c). The tension details given show that 2.6 stitches = 1cm (½in), so multiply 2.6 by the length of the bottom of the shade (c). In our example 2.6 x 56 = 145.60, which can be rounded down to 145 stitches.

• Now calculate the number of rows required to create the height of the shade (b). The tension details given show that 4.1 rows = 1cm (½in), so multiply 4.1 by the height of the shade (b). In our example 4.1 x 15 = 61.5, which can be rounded down to 60 rows.

• Calculate the number of extra stitches that make (d) at each side of the bottom (c). The tension details show that 2.6 stitches = 1cm (½in), so multiply this by the length of (d). In our example, this is 2.6 x 7.5 = 19.5, rounded up to 20 stitches.

• Now calculate the number of stitches to decrease by to get a tightly fitting cover. To do this, divide the rows required for the height of the shade (b) by the extra stitches on each side (d). In our example this is 60/20, which scales down to 3/1. This means that we need to reduce by one stitch at both ends of every third row.

PATTERN

The following pattern could be increased proportionately for a taller shade:

• Work in stocking stitch.
• Main yarn: 2cm (¾in).
• Contrast yarn: 2 rows.
• Main yarn: 1.5cm (½in).
• Contrast yarn: 4 rows.
• Main yarn: 4cm (1½in).
• Contrast yarn: 2 rows.
• Main yarn: 2.5cm (1in).
• Contrast yarn: 2 rows.
• Main yarn: 3cm (1⅛in).

TO MAKE UP

• Press out the knitted section using a steam iron.

• Fold the fabric in half, lining up the stripes so that the 2 edges meet with wrong sides together. Pin the edges into place and close them as neatly as possible using the polycotton thread. Turn the knitting out and press once again.

• Pull the cover on to the shade. *See 3* It should fit snugly, but if necessary sew some small stitches on the top and bottom to secure it. *See 4*

YARN

Main: 1 x 50g (1¾oz) ball Jaeger Trinity, shade 444 Cream

Contrast: 1 x 100g (3½oz) ball Rowan Kid Silk Haze, shade 590 Pearl

NEEDLES

1 pair 3.25mm/UK 10/US 3 needles

TENSION

41 rows x 26 stitches in pattern make a 10cm (4in) square

ADDITIONAL MATERIALS

Lampshade – in the example shown:
height = 15cm (6in)
top circumference = 41cm (16⅛in)
bottom circumference = 56cm (22in)

Lamp base

Polycotton thread to match yarn

Sewing needle

Pins

TIP Take care to use a lampshade that can be covered safely – enclosed shades that could become overheated must be avoided. Never exceed the recommended wattage of the bulb advised for use in the shade.

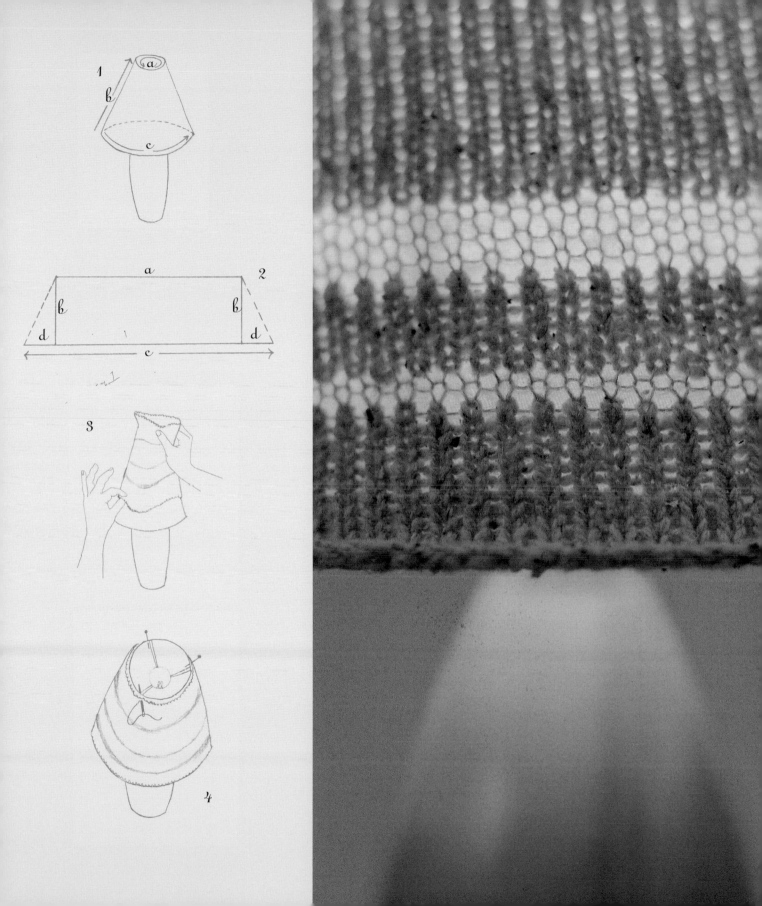

Beanie Hat

These vibrant stripes will cheer up the darkest and coldest of winter days. You can use two contrasting balls of Aran yarn or combine one with another double-wound 4-ply if you prefer more muted colours. The hat is knitted quickly using a circular needle (in the same way as with double-pointed needles, you work in knit only and count where each row begins from the cast-on yarn). Circular knitting also avoids any bulky side seams. Stocking stitch is used throughout, giving the distinctive rolled bottom hem.

PATTERN
Body
- Using stripe-1 yarn, cast on 94 stitches on the 4mm/UK 8/US 6 circular needle using the two-needle method.
- Work 6 rows in knit. *See 1* Work the stitches that close the circle as tightly as possible. The cast-on edge will roll as you work.
- *Change to stripe-2 yarn and knit 6 rows.
Change to stripe-1 yarn and knit 6 rows*.
- Repeat from * to *.
- Change to stripe-2 yarn and work 3 rows before commencing the shaping.
- Next row: **knit 2 tog, knit 4**. Repeat from ** to ** to last 4 stitches, knit 2 tog, knit 2 (leaving 78 stitches).
- Work 2 more rows in stripe-2 yarn.
- Divide the 78 stitches equally between a stitch holder and one of the pair of 4mm/UK 8/US 6 needles. *See 2*

Shaping the top
- Change to stripe-1 yarn and start shaping the first side on the 39 transferred stitches. Working on 2 needles means that stocking stitch must be used (knit when the right side is facing you, purl when the reverse is facing you).
- Next 2 rows: work without shaping.
- Next row: work 2, *work 2 tog, work 4*, repeat from * to * the last 4 stitches, work 2 together, work 2. (30 stitches)

- Next 2 rows: work without shaping.
- Next row: *work 4, work 2 tog*, repeat from * to *. (25 stitches)
- Change to stripe-2 yarn and work the next row without shaping.
- Next row: *work 2 tog, work 3* repeat from * to *. (20 stitches)
- Next row: work without shaping.
- Then repeat the previous 2 rows. (16 stitches)
- Next row: *work 2 tog, work 1* repeat from * to *, knitting the remaining stitches at the end of the row.
- Next row: work without shaping. Repeat the previous shaping row. (7 stitches)
- Leave about 30cm (12in) of yarn before breaking it off.
- Transfer the remaining stitches to the stitch holder.
- Move the stitches for the second side to a 4mm/UK 8/US 6 needle.
- Work the other side of the hat, shaping to match.

TO MAKE UP
- Steam-iron the hat before sewing up one side seam.
- Thread the cast-off yarn from one outside edge through all the remaining stitches. Pull tight and sew the thread into the side seam.
- Sew up the other side seam. *See 3*

YARN
Stripe 1: 1 x 50g (1¾oz) ball Jaeger Matchmaker Merino 4-ply, shade 746 Sundew (rewind to give 2 approximately equal balls)

Stripe 2: 1 x 50g (1¾oz) ball Jaeger Extrafine Merino Aran, shade 551 Pandora

NEEDLES
1 pair 4mm/UK 8/US 6 needles

1 x 40cm (15¾in) circular needle size 4mm/UK 8/US 6

TENSION
Working with 4mm/UK 8/US 6 needles, 30 rows x 19 stitches make a 10cm (4in) square

ADDITIONAL MATERIALS
Large-eye needle for sewing up
Stitch holder or large safety pin

SIZE
18cm (7¼in) height x 25cm (10in) width

1

2

3

Granny's Shopper

This characterful bag is knitted in two contrasting cotton yarns with such a luxuriously soft texture that you'll soon be dreaming up new knitting projects in which to use them. When knitted on large needles, these yarns lie flat and have a strong, elastic quality – ideal for a stretchy but smart 'string' bag. In bright colours and teamed with smooth wooden handles, this bag makes the perfect casual statement on the beach. For a different style, darker colour yarn could be knitted and lined with a toning fabric and matching plastic handles.

PATTERN

- Cast on 14 stitches in the main yarn using the two-needle method and work 6 rows in stocking stitch.
- **Inserting the first handle:** Pick up the 14 cast-on stitches on to the thinner extra needle so that the 2 needles point in the same direction when the work is held in the left hand. See 1a and 1b
- Lay 1 handle on top of the knitting between the 2 needles and knit together through the first stitch on each needle. See 2
- Then knit together each pair of stitches along the row so that the handle is held in place.
- **Shape the bag:** Row 8: purl.
- Row 9: *(knit into the front and back of the first stitch, knit 1)*. Repeat from * to * to the end of the row (a total of 21 stitches).
- Row 10: knit (the very first row of garter trim).
- Row 11: repeat row 9 (giving a total of 32 stitches).
- Row 12: knit (the second row of garter trim). Leave a short length of the main yarn and cut the yarn.
- Row 13: join in contrast yarn and knit.
- Row 14: purl.
- Row 15: knit into the front and back of the first and last stitch of this knit row (a total of 34 stitches). Leave a short length of contrast yarn and cut the yarn.
- Row 16: join in main yarn and purl.
- Row 17: knit.
- Row 18: purl.
- Row 19: knit into the front and back of the first and last stitch of this knit row (a total of 36 stitches).
- Row 20: purl. Leave a short length of the main yarn and cut the yarn.
- Row 21: join in contrast yarn and knit.
- Row 22: purl.
- Row 23: knit. Leave a short length of the contrast yarn and cut the yarn.
- Row 24 to 26: repeat rows 16–18.
- Row 27: knit.
- Row 28: purl. Leave a short length of the main yarn and cut the yarn.
- Row 29 to 31: repeat rows 21–23.
- Row 32: join in main yarn and purl. Decrease 1 stitch at the beginning of the row by purling the first 2 stitches together. Purl to the last 2 stitches; purl these together (a total of 34 stitches).
- Row 33: decrease 1 stitch at the beginning of the row by knitting the first 2 stitches together. Knit to the last 2 stitches; knit these together (a total of 32 stitches).
- Row 34–35: continue in main yarn and repeat rows 32 and 33 (a total of 28 stitches).
- Row 36: continue in main yarn and repeat row 32 (a total of 26 stitches).
- Row 37: continue in main yarn and commence garter trim. Purl.
- Row 38: continue in main yarn. Knit.
- Row 39: continue in main yarn. Purl.
- Row 40: continue in main yarn. Purl, but increase in the first and last stitches (a total of 28 stitches).

YARN

Main: 5 x 50g (1¾oz) balls R2 Rag (100% cotton), shade Z601000.

Contrast: 1 x 50g (1¾oz) ball Jaeger Celeste (viscose/polyamide/linen mix), shade 184 Lobster

NEEDLES

1 pair 12mm/UK 000/US 17 needles

1 extra smaller-sized needle, such as an 8mm/UK 0/US 11

TENSION

No need to check tension when working on such large needles. Use slightly smaller or larger needles if the number of cast-on stitches do not fit snugly round your chosen handle.

ADDITIONAL MATERIALS

A pair of circular wooden handles, external diameter 15.5cm (6in), available from haberdashery departments

Polycotton thread to match main yarn

Sewing needle

Pins

- Row 41: continue in main yarn. Knit, but increase in the first and last stitches (a total of 30 stitches).
- Row 42–43: repeat rows 40 and 41. Leave a short length of main yarn and cut the yarn (a total of 34 stitches).
- Row 44: join in contrast yarn. Purl, but increase in the first and last stitches (a total of 36 stitches).
- Row 45: knit.
- Row 46: purl. Leave a short length of the contrast yarn and cut the yarn.
- Row 47: join in main yarn and knit.
- Row 48: purl.
- Row 49: knit.
- Row 50–51: repeat rows 48 and 49. Leave a short length of the main yarn and cut the yarn.
- Row 52: Join in contrast yarn. Purl.
- Row 53: knit.
- Row 54: purl. Leave a short length of the contrast yarn and cut the yarn.
- Row 55: join in main yarn and knit.
- Row 56: purl.
- Row 57: decrease 1 stitch at the beginning of the row by knitting the first 2 stitches together. Knit to the last two stitches; knit these together (a total of 34 stitches).
- Row 58: purl.
- Row 59: knit. Leave a short length of the main yarn and cut the yarn.
- Row 60: join in contrast yarn. Purl.
- Row 61: decrease 1 stitch at the beginning of the row by knitting the first 2 stitches together. Knit to the last 2 stitches; knit these together (leaving a total of 32 stitches).
- Row 62: purl. Leave a short length of the contrast yarn and cut the yarn.

- Row 63: join in main yarn and knit.
- Row 64: knit (gives garter-trim effect).
- Row 65: *knit 2 together, knit 1*, repeat from * to * (a total of 21 stitches).
- Row 66: knit (gives garter-trim effect).
- Row 67: repeat row 65 (a total of 14 stitches).

Inserting the second handle
- Work 8 rows of stocking stitch.
- With the reverse side of the work facing you, and working so that the extra needle points in the same direction as the 12mm/UK 000/US 17 needle holding the bag, pick up the 14 stitches behind the first garter-trim row.
- Position the handle between the 2 needles and purl together the pairs of stitches from the 2 needles. It is easier to slip the extra needle stitch in front of the 12mm/UK 000/US 17 needle stitch just before purling them together, using the extra needle as a holding device.
- **Cast off:** *Knit 2, pass the first stitch on the needle over the second, knit 1*. Repeat from * to * to the end of the row in order to cast off the remaining stitches.

TO MAKE UP
- Press the bag lightly on the reverse side of the knitting using a steam iron on a flat surface.
- After allowing any residual moisture to evaporate, stitch the side seams with the right sides facing. Use a needle with a double thread and oversew with relatively small stitches – the stitch size varies according to whether you are sewing the main or contrast yarn bands (smaller and neater for the contrast yarn will be necessary!). See 3

1a

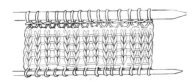

1b

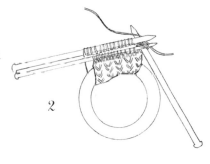

2

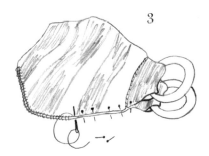

3

Embellished Knits

Spider's-Web Evening Scarf

This scarf is really easy to knit – it uses garter stitch and a luxury yarn embellished with beads and sequins that are threaded on to the yarn before knitting. Worked in a delicate mohair/silk yarn, it is given a light, airy texture by being knitted with needles of two different sizes. The scarf also looks great knitted without beads for more casual wear.

PATTERN

• Before starting to knit, thread the beads randomly on to approximately 3m (10ft) of yarn. The beads must be spread out over the length of yarn, leaving a clear run of yarn at the start and finish, of a rough length of 50cm (20in), to make casting on and off easier. See 1 The beaded yarn is then wound into a ball.
• Cast on 25 stitches using the two-needle method and start knitting with the beaded yarn in combination with the 12mm/UK 000/US 17 needles.
• Row 1: knit.
• Row 2: knit on to the 7mm/UK 2/US 10½ needle.
• Row 3: knit on to the 12mm/UK 000/US 17 needle. See 2

• Rows 2 and 3 form the pattern.
• Change to unbeaded yarn at the beginning of a row after approximately 20cm (8in).
• The scarf shown here was knitted to a total length of 145cm (57in), before joining in the beaded yarn again and knitting the beaded panel to match the other end. You can easily vary the length to suit your own requirements.

TO MAKE UP

Tie the loose yarns together very firmly and snip them off close to the knot. Then press the scarf very lightly with a steam iron.

YARN

1 x 25g (1oz) ball Rowan Kidsilk Haze, shade 589 Majestic

NEEDLES

1 pair 12mm/UK 000/US 17 needles

A single 7mm/UK 2/US 10½ needle

TENSION

No need to check tension when working such an unusual stitch. You could use slightly smaller or larger needles plus a few stitches more or less to achieve a similar look.

ADDITIONAL MATERIALS

Small tub of lightweight pearl sequins (a rough total of 150 beads)

Small tub of lightweight mixed black and silver beads (a rough total of 250–300 beads)

A needle whose eye will pass through the beads

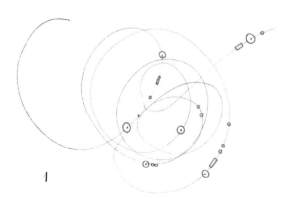

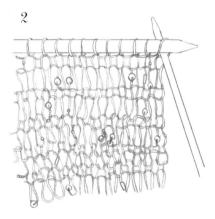

2

1

Pom-Pom Scarf

This versatile scarf is worked entirely in stocking stitch using a light, soft, chunky wool. The fringing is knitted as part of the scarf and the ends of the fringing are decorated with tiny handmade pom-poms. This means that you could try out one of the new pom-pom-making kits (widely available from haberdashery departments), although instructions for the traditional handmade approach are also given here.

PATTERN

Fringe

• Cast on 3 stitches (loop method) in the main yarn and work a 30cm (12in) strip in stocking stitch (knit 1 row, purl 1 row and then repeat for the required number of rows). The last row worked should be a purl row. Leave a short length of the main yarn attached before breaking it off.

• Leave the strip on the needle (or move it to a smaller-size needle) while you work 4 more strips to the following lengths: 15cm (6in), 21cm (8¼in), 19cm (7½in) and 30cm (12in).

• Arrange the 5 strips across the left-hand needle so that the smooth-knit side of the fabric is facing you, ready to join them together. The 30cm (12in) strips should be on the outside edges. See 1

• Joining row: *knit 2, knit into front and back of stitch*, repeat from * to * 3 times, knit 3. You have now increased the stitches to a total of 19. See 2

Body

• From the join, work 5cm (2in) in stocking stitch, commencing with a purl row. Do not break the main yarn but join in the first double-stranded contrast yarn, starting on a knit row, and work 2 rows.

• Work 5cm (2in) in the main yarn, 2 rows of the second contrast yarn and then an additional 5cm (2in) in the main yarn.

• Work just 1 row of the third contrast yarn on a knit row, neatly catching in the main yarn on the reverse side.

• Continue in the main yarn until the scarf measures 50cm (20in) from the joining row. Work 1 row in the third contrast colour as before, then complete the main/contrast yarn pattern to match the opposite end of the scarf. End with a purl row.

Second fringe

• Knit 3 and turn the work to purl back on these 3 stitches, leaving the rest of the original row on the needle. Continue working the 3 stitches until a 30cm (12in) strip has been worked. Break off the yarn and rejoin for the next strip.

• Knit 2, pass the first stitch over the second stitch, knit 2. Turn and purl 3.

• Continue until the second strip is 15cm (6in) long. See 3 Repeat so that the third to fifth strips are 21cm (8¼in), 19cm (7½in), and 30cm (12in) long.

YARN

Main: 1 x 100g (3½oz) ball Rowan Polar wool, shade 640 Stony

Contrast 1: 1 x 50g (1¾oz) ball Jaeger Baby Merino wool 4-ply, shade 094 Red Cheek

Contrast 2: 1 x 50g (1¾oz) ball Jaeger Baby Merino DK, shade 228 Flannel

Contrast 3: 1 x 50g (1¾oz) ball Jaeger Baby Merino wool 4-ply, shade 096 Marigold.

Wind each contrast colour into 2 balls so that the yarns can be used double-stranded.

NEEDLES

1 pair 8mm/UK 0/US 11 needles

TENSION

16 rows x 12 stitches make a 10cm (4in) square

TO FINISH

Large-eye sewing needle

3.5cm (1½in) diameter pom-pom maker (available from larger haberdashery departments) or alternatively use the handmade method described here.

Plaited Belt

Quick and simple to make, this funky belt combines well with jeans or it can be worn low on the hips with a dress or skirt. The loose, open knit means the strips of knitting grow rapidly, so you can experiment with different yarn and colour combinations to enhance your wardrobe. By altering the width of the strips, you could create anything from a pencil-thin belt to a really chunky wrap.

PATTERN
• Measure the final length of belt that you require and double it – this allows extra fabric for plaiting and overlap.
• Work 3 equal strips to the required length in loose stocking stitch, using a different colour yarn for each strip. The strips were 8 stitches wide for the belt shown in the example opposite.

TO MAKE UP
• Press the strips out without undue concern over the rolling edges – the yarn only needs to be relaxed.

• Place the strips one on top of the other and sew them together using the yarn colour of the top strip. *See 1*
• Plait the 3 strips together and neatly secure the ends. *See 2*
• Take the belt buckle, feed the plait through and push through the bar. Sew down the ends. *See 3*
• A belt loop can be made by knitting several stitches in stocking stitch on fine needles until the length will go round the plait. Cast off, sew the ends together and secure them at the back of the belt with a few stitches. *See 4*

YARN
A: 1 x 50g (1¾oz) ball Jaeger Mohair Art, shade 606 Blue Boy

B: 1 x 50g (1¾oz) ball Jaeger Mohair Art, shade 602 Blue Haze

C: 1 x 50g (1¾oz) ball Rowan Kid Classic, shade 835 Royal

NEEDLES
For yarns A and B: 4mm/ UK 8/US 6 needles

For yarn C: 5–5.5mm/UK 5–6/ US 8–9 needles

TENSION
No need to check tension as this is an experimental piece of knitting. Change the needle size if you don't like the look of the pattern once you've started the first strip.

ADDITIONAL MATERIALS
Belt buckle (from a haberdashery store, or recycle an old one by cutting off the leather or fabric)

Polycotton thread to match yarn

Sewing needle

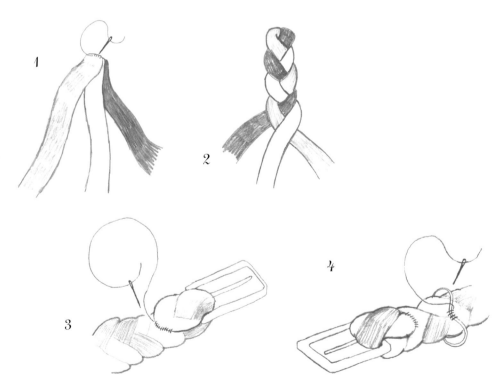

Textured Knits

Panelled Baby Blanket

A hand-knitted baby blanket must be one of the most appreciated of gifts for a new mum, but it can be hard to find time to knit such a large item. This blanket is worked in panels using unusual stitches, which are challenging but easy to learn. The whole piece comes together at the making-up stage, so you can pop an individual panel in a bag to work on when you have a spare moment. The one shown overleaf uses neutral colours, but it would also be fun to use bright reds with orange and yellow highlights, or soft pastels for a more traditional style.

PATTERN
Panel 1
• Cast on 44 stitches using yarn A and 4mm/UK 8/US 6 needles. Work 20cm (8in) in the pattern shown below. End the pattern at row 4. If your tension looks too tight/loose on this stitch you should change the size of needles for the whole panel. Width changes will be very slight.
Panel 1 pattern:
  • Row 1: knit.
  • Row 2: knit 2 together, all across the row.
  • Row 3: knit into the front and back of each stitch.
  • Row 4: purl.
• Change to yarn B and continue the pattern for a further 13cm (5in), ending after completing row 2 of the pattern, leaving you with 22 stitches. The total length of the knitting should now be 33cm (13in).
• Change to yarn C and 5mm/UK 6/US 8 needles, combining 2 strands of the yarn together to give a thicker fabric.
• Work 6 rows of stocking stitch.
• Change to yarn D and continue in garter stitch until panel 1 is 75cm (30in) long.
• Having completed this first panel, make two more to match.
Panel 2
• Lace band: 30 x 30cm (12 x 12in) – 2 required
• Waffle band: 25 x 30cm (10 x 12in) – 2 required
• Garter band: 15 x 30cm (6 x 12in) – 2 required

• Lace band: Cast on 34 stitches using 2 strands of yarn E and 5mm/UK 6/ US 8 needles.
• Change to 7.5mm/UK 1/US 11 needles, purl 1 row and start the pattern as follows.
• Lace band pattern:
  • Row 1: purl.
  • Row 2: knit 1, *yarn round needle, knit 2 together, knit 1)*, repeat from * to * to last stitch, knit 1. See 1
  • Row 3: purl.
  • Row 4: purl.
• Waffle band: Cast on 26 stitches using 2 strands of yarn F and 7.5mm/UK 1/ US 11 needles.
• Work in the pattern below until the band is 30cm (12in) long, ending with a waffle side row. See 2a and 2b
• Waffle band pattern:
  • Rows 1–2: knit.
  • Row 3: *knit 1, knit 1 below* (Insert the right-hand needle through the centre of the loop just below the next stitch and then take the yarn round the needle as for a normal knit stitch.) Repeat from * to * along the row.
  • Row 4: *pick up the long (top) yarn produced by the knit 1 below and knit it together with the stitch on the needle. Knit 1*. Repeat from * to * along the row.
  • Row 5: *knit 1 below, knit 1*. Repeat from * to * along the row.
  • Row 6: *knit 1, pick up the long (top) yarn produced by the knit 1 below and knit it together with the stitch on the needle, in the same way as row 4*.

YARN

A: 3 x 50g (1¾oz) balls Jaeger Baby Merino DK, shade SH0203 Pearl

B: 4 x 50g (1¾oz) balls Jaeger Baby Merino DK, shade SH188 Choco

C: 2 x 50g (1¾oz) balls Jaeger Aqua Cotton, shade SH303 Herb

D: 3 x 50g (1¾oz) balls Jaeger Extrafine Merino Chunky, shade SH021 Pearl

E: 4 x 50g (1¾oz) balls Jaeger Merino Double Knitting, shade SH662 Cream

F: 4 x 50g (1¾oz) balls Jaeger Merino Double Knitting, shade SH663 Light Natural

G: 1 x 50g (1¾oz) ball Jaeger Alpaca 4-ply, shade SH390 Crush, rewound into 2 smaller balls

NEEDLES

1 pair 4mm/UK 8/US 6 needles

1 pair 5mm /UK 6/US 8 needles

1 pair 7.5mm/UK 1/US 11 needles

TENSION

This pattern can accommodate slight variations in tension. Use your judgement after working the first panel and adjust the needle size appropriately.

ADDITIONAL MATERIALS

Large-eye needle for sewing up

Repeat from * to * along the row.
- Row 7: knit one row.
- Cast off loosely in knit.
- Garter band: Cast on 16 stitches using two strands of yarn B and 7.5mm/UK 1/ US 11 needles.
- Work in garter stitch (all rows knit) until the panel is 15cm (6in) long.
- Garter band pattern:
  - Pick up and knit 63 stitches along one of the long edges of the rectangle using 2 strands of yarn G and 4mm/UK 8/ US 6 needles.

- Work 4cm (1½in) in stocking stitch (knit 1 row, purl 1 row).
- Cast off loosely in knit.

TO MAKE UP
- Steam-iron all the pieces and sew up the seams with the right sides facing using matching yarns. See 3
- Trim any remaining short lengths of yarn from the panels and sew them into the seams.

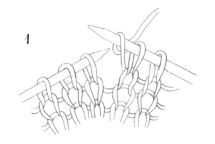

1

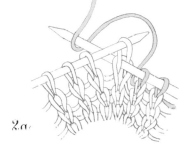

2a

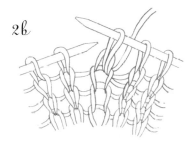

2b

panel 1   panel 2   panel 1

a   e   d   b   g   a

b   f   e   f   b

c   b   c

d   g   b   a   e   d

3

panel 1   panel 2

Open-Stitch Fringed Poncho

This sophisticated poncho is knitted in ultra-soft yarns, both plain and marled, in subtle tones of grey and black. The light weight of the garment is deceptive because the use of an open stitch and a wide fringe combine to keep the wearer snug and warm. The poncho is worked as two halves and two strands of yarn are worked together for a speedier knit – well, what are you waiting for?

PATTERN

- Work with both strands of yarn from each 2 balls of wool for every colour change.
- Neck: Cast on 35 stitches using stripe-1 yarn. Work 10 rows in stocking stitch (row 1: knit, row 2: purl).
- Commence working in pattern:
- Row 1: knit 3, *(yarn to front, knit 2 tog, knit 1)*. Repeat from * to * to the last 2 stitches, knit 2.
- Row 2: row 2 and all subsequent even rows, purl.
- Rows 3–4: repeat rows 1 and 2.
- Row 5: knit twice into the first stitch, knit 2, *(yarn to front, knit 2 tog, knit 1)*.
- Repeat from * to * to the last 2 stitches, knit 1, knit twice into the last stitch.
- Row 6: increase by 1 stitch at either end of the row.
- Row 7: knit twice into the first stitch, knit 1, *(yarn to front, knit 2 tog, knit 1)*.
- Repeat from * to * to the last stitch, knit twice into the last stitch.

- Row 8: increase 1 stitch at either end of row.
- Row 9: knit twice into the first stitch *(yarn to front, knit 2 tog, knit 1)*. Repeat from * to * to the last 3 stitches, yarn to front, knit 2 tog, knit twice into the last stitch.
- Row 10: increase by 1 stitch at either end of the row.
- Increases are now worked at either end of the knit rows only.
- Row 11: change to stripe-2 yarn. Work 10 rows in pattern, increasing by 1 stitch at either end of the knit rows.
- Row 21: change to stripe-3 yarn. Work 10 rows in pattern, increasing by 1 stitch at either end of the knit rows.
- Row 31: change to stripe-4 yarn. Work 10 rows in pattern, increasing by 1 stitch at either end of the knit rows.
- Row 41: change to stripe-5 yarn. Work 10 rows in pattern, increasing by 1 stitch at either end of the knit rows.
- Row 51: cast off.
- Work the second side in the same way.

YARN

Neck and stripe 1: 2 x 50g (1¾oz) balls Jaeger Extrafine Merino Double Knitting, shade 978 Coal Dust

Stripe 2: 2 x 50g (1¾oz) balls Jaeger Extrafine Merino Double Knitting, shade 951 Jet

Stripe 3: 2 x 50g (1¾oz) balls Jaeger Extrafine Merino Double Knitting, shade 959 Charcoal

Stripe 4: 2 x 50g (1¾oz) balls Jaeger Extrafine Merino Double Knitting, shade 977 Badger

Stripe 5: 2 x 50g (1¾oz) balls Jaeger Extrafine Merino Double Knitting, shade 942 Flannel

Stripe 5: 2 x 50g (1¾oz) balls Jaeger Extrafine Merino Double Knitting, shade 976 Ash

Fringe: 2 x 50g (1¾oz) balls Jaeger Extrafine Merino Double Knitting, shade 941 Smoke

NEEDLES

1 pair 5mm /UK 6/US 8 needles

TENSION

Working in stocking stitch 24 rows by 14 stitches make a 10cm (4in) square.

ADDITIONAL MATERIALS

A sheet of sturdy cardboard, length 30cm (12in)

Large-eye needle for sewing up

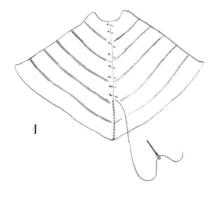

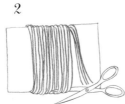

TO MAKE UP

• Steam-iron both pieces of the poncho on a flat surface, making sure that the pattern holes are kept vertical.

• Lay the 2 pieces together with right sides facing and then join the stripe seams with matching yarn. *See 1* The roll-neck seam should be worked on the right side of the fabric and the roll secured on the right side with a neat stitch.

MAKING THE FRINGE

• Prepare the fringe by winding the fringe yarn around a sturdy 30cm (12in) wide piece of card (the length of the card doesn't matter). *See 2*

• To create lengths that are 60cm (24in) long, cut the yarn along one edge of the wound yarn. Then batch together 5 strands of yarn and fold them in half.

• Push the end loop through one of the pattern holes on the cast-off edge, working from the reverse side. Pull the yarn ends through the loop as tightly as possible. *See 3* Repeat until each of the pattern holes along the bottom of the poncho has been fringed

Wool-Slub Cushion

This classic and yet also highly contemporary cushion is knitted in a luxurious 100 per cent Merino wool slub yarn. The chunky yarn creates an uneven textured fabric that grows rapidly using large needles with simple stocking stitch. A decorative cast-off edge is obtained using another 100 per cent wool yarn – this matches the other one in colour but has a much smoother texture. The cushion requires only two seams, quickly handsewn together to finish.

PATTERN

• Cast on 30 stitches in main yarn and work 90cm (36in) in stocking stitch, starting with a knit row. See 1
• Cast off using the cast-off yarn to give a neat finish.

TO MAKE UP

• With right sides of the fabric facing, fold in the cast-off edge by 25cm (10in) and pin into position. See 2
• Pull the cast-off edge across, ensuring that it is anchored securely at each side.

It is better to overlap the cast-off edge over the side edge to give a tighter fit for the cushion pad. Sew up the cushion using a length of cast-off yarn.
• Then fold in the cast-on edge by 25cm (10in) so that it overlaps with the cast-off side. Pin into position, as far as possible, and sew as before.
• Now turn the cushion to the right side and insert the cushion pad. See 3

YARN

Main: 5 x 100g (3½oz) balls Rowan Biggy Print Z014000, shade 258 Sheep

Cast-off yarn: 1 x 50g (1¾oz) ball Jaeger Extrafine Merino Chunky, shade 021 Pearl

NEEDLES

1 pair 12mm/UK 000/US 17 needles

TENSION

9 rows by 7 stitches make a 10cm (4in) square.

ADDITIONAL MATERIALS

40 x 40cm (15¾ x 15¾in) cushion pad

Large-eye needle for sewing up

Pins

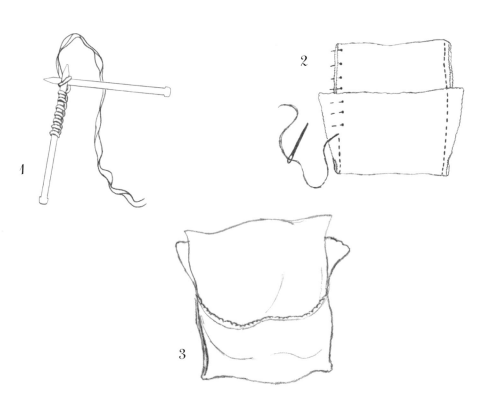

Addresses

ANGEL YARNS
PO Box 153
Hove, Sussex
BN3 6UZ
01273 411112
www.angelyarns.com
Rowan stockist

ANTIQUE CRAFTS
276 West Wycombe Road,
High Wycombe, Bucks, HP12 4AB
01494 447514
www.antiquecrafts.co.uk
Mail-order supplier of craft products,
offering a huge range of buttons, lace,
beads, embellishments and trimmings

BARNYARNS
Canal Wharf, Bondgate Green,
Ripon, North Yorkshire, HG4 1BR
0870 870 8586
www.barnyarns.com
Extensive sewing and embroidery
mail-order supplies

THE BEAD SHOP
21a Tower Street,
London, WC2H 9NS
020 7240 0931
www.beadworks.co.uk
All types of beads, including
semi-precious stones

THE BERWICK STREET CLOTH SHOP
14 Berwick Street, London, W1F 0PP
020 7287 2881
Comprehensive range of fabrics
from wool to silk

THE BUTTON QUEEN
19 Marylebone Lane,
London, W1V 2NF
020 7935 1505
www.thebuttonqueen.co.uk
Every type of button you can
imagine and more!

BUY MAIL LTD
01234 838303
www.buy-mail.com
sales@buy-mail.com
Online Rowan stockist

COLOURWAY
Market Street
Whitland
Carmarthenshire
Wales
SA34 0AJ
01994 241333
www.colourway.co.uk
shop@colourway.co.uk
Rowan stockist

CRAFT DEPOT
Somerton Business Park,
Somerton, Somerset, TA11 6SB
01458 274727
www.craftdepot.co.uk
Mail-order craft supplies

CRAFTY RIBBONS
3 Beechwood Clump Farm,
Tin Pot Lane, Blandford,
Dorset, DT11 7TD
01258 455889
www.craftyribbons.com
Ribbon emporium

GET KNITTED
Bristol
0117 941 2600
www.getknitted.com
Rowan stockist with online catalogue

HOBBY CRAFT
Forbury Retail Park, Off Kenavon
Drive, Reading, Berkshire, RG1 3HS
0118 902 8600
For store locations call:
0800 027 2387
www.hobbycraft.co.uk
Craft materials and equipment

HOME CRAFTS DIRECT
0116 269 7733
www.homecraftsdirect.co.uk
Mail-order craft materials

JOHN LEWIS
Oxford Street
London
W1A 1EX
020 7629 7711
The haberdashery department
stocks all types of knitting yarns and
accessories. Check the website for
store locations nationwide

KANGAROO
PO Box 43, Lewes
East Sussex
BN8 5YT
01273 814900
www.kangaroo.uk.com
sales@kangaroo.uk.com
Rowan stockist with worldwide
mail-order service

KLEINS
5 Noel Street
London
W1F 8GD
020 7437 6162
www.kleins.co.uk
Craft and haberdashery suppliers,
extensive range of bag handles
available by mail order

LAUGHING HENS
PO Box 176
St Leonards-on-Sea
East Sussex
0870 770 4352
www.laughinghens.com
Knitting supplies and Rowan stockist

LIBERTY
210–220 Regent Street
London
W1R 5AH
020 7734 1234
Haberdashery department for knitting
yarn, and accessories

MCAREE BROS LTD
55–59 King Street
Stirling, Scotland
FK8 1DR
01786 465646
www.mcadirect.com
Knitting yarns and patterns

PENTONVILLE RUBBER
104 Pentonville Road
Islington
London
N1 9JB
020 7837 7553
www.pentonvillerubber.co.uk
Stockist of upholstery foam, can cut
shapes to your specifications

PONGEES
28–30 Hoxton Square,
London, N1 6NN
020 7739 9130
www.pongees.co.uk
Specializes in silk and offer a huge
range; mail order service available

ROWAN YARNS
Green Lane Mill
Holmfirth
HD9 2DX
01484 681881
www.knitrowan.com
Website also has an international
stockists directory

SHOREHAM KNITTING
19 East Street
Shoreham-by-Sea
West Sussex
BN43 5ZE
01273 461029
www.englishyarns.co.uk
sales@englishyarns.co.uk
Online knitting store and
Rowan stockist

UP COUNTRY
78 Huddersfield Road
Holmfirth
West Yorkshire
HD9 3AZ
01484 687803
www.upcountry.co.uk
info@upcountry.co.uk
Rowan stockist

**THE VOIRREY EMBROIDERY
CENTRE**
Brimstage Hall, Brimstage,
Wirral, CH63 6JA
0151 3423514
www.voirrey.com
Textile, needlework and knitting
stockists and mail order suppliers

YARN FORWARD
247 Westbrook Road
Unit 1, Carp, Ontario
K0A 1L0 Canada
+1 (613) 831 9673
www.yardforward.com
Mail-order stockist for all knitting,
crochet and needlecraft supplies

Index